This book is due for return on or before the date last
stamped below unless an extension of time is granted

2196

AFRICANS

in America

Ayanna Hart and Earl Spangler

 Lerner Publications Company • Minneapolis

Front cover: Martin Luther King Day parade, New York City

Copyright © 1995 by Lerner Publications Company

1995 REVISED EDITION

Library of Congress Cataloging-in-Publication Data

Hart, Ayanna.
  Africans in America / by Ayanna Hart and Earl Spangler.
    p. cm. — (In America)
  Includes index.
  ISBN 0-8225-1952-6 (hardcover)
  ISBN 0-8225-3476-2 (pbk.)
  1. Afro-Americans—History—Juvenile literature. [1. Afro-Americans—History.] I. Spangler, Earl. II. Spangler, Earl. Negro in America. III. Title. IV. Series: In America (Minneapolis, Minn.)
E185.H32 1995
973'.0496073 — dc20   94-33873

Manufactured in the United States of America

1 2 3 4 5 6 – I/M – 00 99 98 97 96 95

CONTENTS ▨▧▨▧▨▧▨

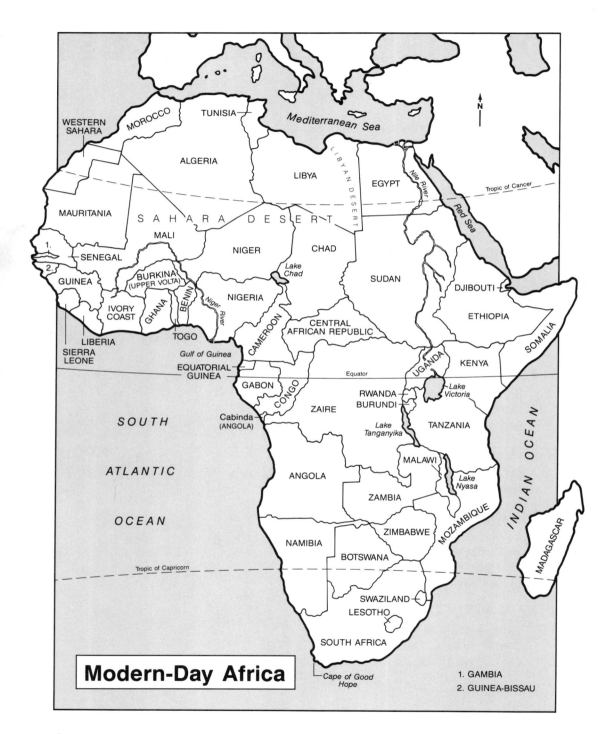

Modern-Day Africa

WESTERN SAHARA
MOROCCO
TUNISIA
Mediterranean Sea
N
ALGERIA
LIBYA
EGYPT
Nile River
Tropic of Cancer
MAURITANIA
S A H A R A   D E S E R T
LIBYAN DESERT
Red Sea
MALI
1.
SENEGAL
2.
NIGER
CHAD
Lake Chad
SUDAN
DJIBOUTI
GUINEA
BURKINA (UPPER VOLTA)
NIGERIA
ETHIOPIA
IVORY COAST
GHANA
BENIN
Niger River
LIBERIA
TOGO
CAMEROON
CENTRAL AFRICAN REPUBLIC
SOMALIA
SIERRA LEONE
Gulf of Guinea
EQUATORIAL GUINEA
UGANDA
KENYA
Equator
GABON
CONGO
RWANDA
Lake Victoria
SOUTH
Cabinda (ANGOLA)
ZAIRE
BURUNDI
Lake Tanganyika
TANZANIA
INDIAN OCEAN
ATLANTIC
MALAWI
ANGOLA
Lake Nyasa
OCEAN
ZAMBIA
MOZAMBIQUE
MADAGASCAR
ZIMBABWE
NAMIBIA
BOTSWANA
SWAZILAND
LESOTHO
SOUTH AFRICA
Tropic of Capricorn
Cape of Good Hope

1. GAMBIA
2. GUINEA-BISSAU

1
AN ANCIENT HOMELAND

A ship sails smoothly through the night, its sails slowly billowing as it pulls out of its docks from the Guinea Coast of West Africa. The vessel, loaded with wares of grain and gold, is making its usual trip to a far-off land, the exotic Americas.

The people of ancient Mexico and other Central and South American nations were used to visitors from distant lands—namely from Africa. These visitors brought the wares of their countries with them to exchange for articles such as clay, pottery, and corn. Some Africans who made the voyage stayed in the Americas.

Enormous stone sculptures of warriors stand along the coast of Mexico. Generally thought to be created by the Olmec Indians, these warriors bear an unmistakable likeness to a different group of people. Their headdresses and faces look like those of Africans. For years scholars have doubted that Africa was home to advanced, seafaring civilizations. The sculptures in Mexico revised their theories. Many scholars now believe that Africans might have traveled to the Americas thousands of years ago, long before Europeans brought Africans to America as slaves.

This sculpture from Mexico suggests that African people might have traveled to the Americas in ancient times.

Cities of Splendor

In ancient times, various African countries were leaders in world trade, science, and philosophical ideas that shaped other cultures. The ancient Egyptians built the first library in the world—the great library of Alexandria—created the world's first national government, developed a 365-day calendar, and built great cities and pyramids. They flourished in northeast Africa from about 2700 to 1070 B.C.

The Nubians, living south of Egypt in the Sudan region, also had an advanced civilization. Their trade empire extended across many lands—to other African nations, Asia, and perhaps even Mexico. Their record of world travel and trade is legendary in African folklore. The Nubians were fiercely competitive with the Egyptians. Both groups wanted to control the Nile River and its banks, which in those days were bountiful with produce and vegetation. The two empires vied for power many times.

The Kush civilization, which developed in the Sudan around 1000 B.C., was a mixture of many cultures. Kush palaces and tombs were Roman in design, yet the Kush took their style of government from the Egyptians. The Kush were also influenced by their neighbors to the northeast in Arabia. The queen of Sheba (an ancient country in southern Arabia) came to the Sudan to hold court with the Kush, and they also had ties with the Christian world. A biblical reference in the Acts of the Apostles states: "And the Apostle Philip encountered and baptized a Kushite dignitary on the road which goeth from Jerusalem to Gaza."

The Arabians brought the Islamic (Muslim) religion to Africa in about A.D. 600, and to this day Islam remains a major African religion. In the 14th century, Mali, a Muslim state, was the most powerful empire in West Africa. Emperor Mansa Musa, who ruled from 1312 to 1332, brought Mali to the height of its power. His empire extended across present-day Gambia, Guinea, and Senegal. Under Mansa Musa, Timbuktu, Mali, became one of the world's greatest cities, renowned for its wealth and splendor. It was home to a university and the largest book trade in the world. After Emperor Musa's death, Mali diminished as a shining star in Africa.

Many great African societies treated the lower classes as did other powerful empires. Just as the ancient Romans kept servants and slaves, so did the Africans. Many people think that slavery didn't appear in Africa until the Europeans arrived. This is untrue. Slaves and

The Egyptians left a vast cultural legacy, including elaborate statues and the giant pyramids.

servants built the Great Pyramids of Egypt. The Nubians practiced slavery in the royal court as well as in upper-class homes. Some African slaves were prisoners of war. Others sold themselves into servitude as a way to pay off their debts.

Slavery was not just an economic arrangement in Africa but also a form of protection. Slaves worked for the king or the chief of a community, who in exchange cared for the slave's family. Slaves were often well-loved and respected household members. Africans did not raid villages just to obtain servants and slaves. They did not shackle their slaves—until the Europeans arrived. Then slave-trading became an organized business enterprise.

Invaders from the North

Africa has many agricultural and mineral riches, including palm oil, peanuts, cocoa, cotton, rubber, gold, diamonds, copper, and petroleum. All of these products

Timbuktu, Mali, as drawn by a French explorer in the 1800s

9

have the potential to bring in large amounts of money for those who harvest or mine them. Ancient Africans traded heavily in gold. But diamonds, found in what is now South Africa, were not deemed very valuable—until Europeans came to Africa.

The development of advanced weaponry (cannons, rifles, and explosives) during the 15th century gave the Europeans an advantage over the Africans. Whenever Africans had faced invaders before (such as the Romans during the first century), they had been able to defend themselves with armies and weapons equal to those of the Europeans. Now, not only were Europeans invading with more powerful weapons, they also came with the teachings of their religion, Christianity.

Portugal was one of the first European countries to send settlers to Africa, with plans to establish colonies and convert the native people to the Christian faith. In the mid-1400s, the Portuguese landed in West Africa, hoping to profit from the gold mines there and to discover a trade route to India around the African coast. They were successful in setting up colonies and converting some Africans to Christianity.

The people of Africa became merely another resource in the eyes of many Europeans— another commodity that could be traded.

Dutch settlers established themselves on the west coast of Africa in the early 1600s. Less than a century later, the Dutch clashed with the Portuguese, who had taken land that the Dutch wanted for themselves. Worried that their trading relationship with India was being taken over by the Portuguese, the Dutch sent Jan van Riebeeck to the Cape of Good Hope at the southern tip of Africa. There, Riebeeck set up a supply base to outfit ships on their long journey from Europe to India.

Soon other Dutch people began to settle in South Africa. They farmed the land, worked the mines, and sold supplies to ships that passed by. A colony developed, and the Afrikaners, as the Dutch and other Europeans were called, soon controlled the region. Their need for labor grew, and they hired black South Africans to work the gold and diamond mines.

The miners received low pay for their work and endured cruel treatment. At the end of each day, miners were searched thoroughly by an overseer. Any African

who had taken even the smallest piece of uncut, un-finished diamond received severe punishment. In more than one instance, African workers were shot and killed.

Portuguese missionaries erect a cross at Cape Town, South Africa.

Europeans also wanted to explore the African conti-nent. The wildlife, varied terrain, and other natural wonders of Africa seemed almost mystical to the new-comers. The English were particularly interested in the African landscape, and by 1553 they had explored Gambia and the Gold Coast along the Gulf of Guinea. They did not venture into the interior of Africa until two centuries later.

The first recorded attempt at a systematic explora-tion of Africa was undertaken by the Africa Associa-tion, a club made up of English scholars and scientists. In 1788 the association decided to explore the Niger River and hired a Scottish doctor, Mungo Park, to under-take the journey. He made two attempts, in 1795 and 1805. Although he never explored the entire river, he

traveled a full 1,200 miles before drowning on his second trip. Two Englishmen later made the full journey in 1830.

The next challenge was the Nile River. No European knew the principal source of the river, and the British Royal Geographical Society sent explorers to find it. They reached Lake Ukerewe in 1858. In 1860 the Europeans renamed it Lake Victoria.

Captured Africans are led in shackles to a coastal slave market.

Why couldn't the Europeans be satisfied with just exploring Africa? Why did they feel the need to pillage all of its assets? The continent of Africa held mysteries for many European people. But perhaps greed overtook their curiosity. Every resource that Africa had was tapped—including its people, who were taken from their homes and families and sold into slavery. The people of Africa became merely another resource in the eyes of many Europeans—another commodity that could be traded.

West African nations provided most of the slaves for the Atlantic slave trade. Numerous tribal groups, such as the Fulani and the Yoruba, dominated the region. Each group had its own unique culture, traditions, and religious practices. African people commonly lived in extended family groups. Each tribe was headed by a chief, who was considered royalty, as was his family.

Often, different African tribes lived in harmony. At other times, tribes warred intensely over territory. During the 1500s, some tribes began to sell off captured rivals to white slave traders. Many Africans captured and sold in such situations found themselves on slave ships headed for the Americas. They often left Africa through the infamous "Door of No Return" from the House of Slaves, a slave-trading station on Goree Island off the coast of Senegal.

During the era of the slave trade, from the early 1500s to the mid-1800s, about 12 million African people were sold into slavery. Two million of these captives died during the ocean voyage to America. Most of the survivors were sold in the slave markets of Brazil or the Caribbean. Approximately six percent (600,000) went to North America—to the British colonies and the future United States.

The first Africans in America came from many different tribes, regions, and cultures. They spoke different languages and dialects. In America, though, they would be united—if only in being black, African, and slaves. Once in America, the Africans began a long struggle for freedom. In many ways, that struggle continues to this day.

2
PEOPLE IN CHAINS

In 1619 a Dutch ship captain sailed into Jamestown, Virginia, and offered to trade 20 Africans to the English settlers there in return for provisions. These first Africans in North America were not considered slaves. They were indentured servants who would work for some years and then be given their freedom. Although slavery was already commonplace in the West Indies—the islands of the Caribbean Sea—it was not then practiced in the North American colonies.

Little by little, however, the rights of Africans in North America were taken away. Although some black Americans retained their freedom, by the mid-18th century, slavery was practiced throughout the colonies. As colonial America grew, so did the demand for slave labor. Slave trading became a profitable business, as many New England merchants exchanged rum, molasses, and other products for African slaves.

The slave's passage to the Americas was marked by suffering and cruelty. Some Africans were kidnapped by white slave traders and taken in shackles to Africa's ports. Other captives were sold to slave traders by rival tribes. From Africa's slave markets, the captives endured a wretched voyage across the Atlantic Ocean. Slave ships were filthy and overcrowded. Food was usually rotten. Water was foul and in short supply.

Many captives would die of disease or starvation before they reached America. So slave ship captains carried a large human cargo. The captives were packed in so tightly below deck that they often couldn't move. Even though many passengers would die, enough Africans would survive the voyage to make the trip worthwhile for the slave traders. Those passengers

Slaves were considered property—with no legal rights or freedoms.

who did survive were brought to Brazil, the West Indies, or to North American ports such as New Orleans and Charleston, where they were then sold to landowners or slave brokers.

A New Nation

By the time of the Revolutionary War with Great Britain (1775–1783), many Americans disapproved of slavery. Some people thought slavery was impractical from

American colonists used slave labor to operate their farms and plantations.

an economic standpoint, while others opposed the practice on religious or ethical grounds. Many Americans believed that the right to "life, liberty, and the pursuit of happiness," as put forth in the Declaration of Independence, should apply to people of all races.

In fact, one of the first men to fall in the struggle for independence was Crispus Attucks, an African American killed by the British during the Boston Massacre of 1770. During the Revolutionary War itself, about 5,000 black men (some slaves, some free men) served in the colonial army and navy. As a result of this service, some slaves were awarded their freedom. Others never returned to their owners after the war.

George Washington (second from right) is shown in this painting as a prosperous slave owner.

The slavery debate heated up at the Constitutional Convention in 1787. Several southern states refused to join the Union unless slavery was permitted in the new nation. As a compromise, the framers of the Constitution agreed not to impose any restrictions on slavery. But they did insist that Congress have the right to forbid the importation of slaves after 1808. Ironically, some early American leaders who claimed to oppose slavery, including George Washington and Thomas Jefferson, were slave owners.

Slavery was never widespread in the North, and most northern states had outlawed slavery by the beginning of the 19th century. The slave trade was outlawed by Congress in March 1807, and the law took effect on January 1, 1808. From then on, slavery increased only as African-American slaves had children, although an illegal slave trade continued well into the 19th century.

By and large, the slavery system was concentrated on plantations in the American South. Southern plantations were large agricultural estates that grew tobacco, rice, sugarcane, and other crops. Perhaps the South's most important crop was cotton. A decade after the Revolutionary War, in 1793, Eli Whitney invented the cotton gin. With this machine, cotton production increased dramatically in the United States and so did the demand for slave labor. Many plantation owners believed they could not run profitable estates without slaves.

TO BE SOLD, on board the Ship *Bance-Island*, on tuesday the 6th of *May* next, at *Asley-Ferry*; a choice cargo of about 250 fine healthy NEGROES, juſt arrived from the Windward & Rice Coaſt. —The utmoſt care has already been taken, and ſhall be continued, to keep them free from the leaſt danger of being infected with the SMALL-POX, no boat having been on board, and all other communication with people from *Charles-Town* prevented.
Auſtin, Laurens, & Appleby.

N. B. Full one Half of the above Negroes have had the SMALL-POX in their own Country.

Life in Bondage

A small number of American slaves worked in cities and towns. Some became skilled craftspeople—tailors, shoemakers, painters, blacksmiths, and carpenters. Others were household servants, factory workers, and laborers.

But most slaves (about 90 percent) worked as plantation hands. Their lives were often brutal. Plantation owners—or masters—had complete control over their slaves' lives. Overseers supervised the slaves' day-to-day

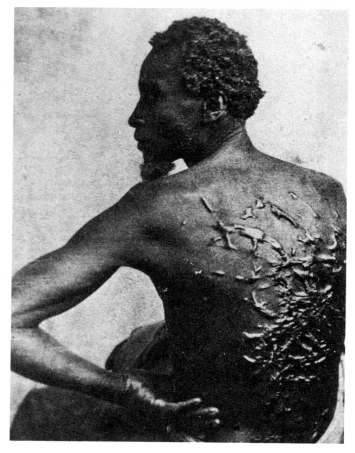

A slave displays his scarred back, the result of years of brutal floggings.

work, often cruelly. Men, women, and children performed backbreaking farmwork, with harsh punishment for those who disobeyed or failed to keep pace.

In what little time they had to themselves, slaves were subjected to strict codes. These were laws passed by various states and counties and enforced by local sheriffs. Slaves who defied the codes received severe punishment—and sometimes death. In general, slaves could not carry weapons, gather in large crowds, marry whites, testify against whites in court, or enter into a legal contract. In some places, laws prohibited slaves from learning to read and write. Usually, slaves could not choose their own spouses, travel alone, or leave the plantation without permission.

Slaves could be bought, sold, or traded as their masters desired. They could not defend themselves against attack. They were often denied religious services. Female slaves were frequently sexually abused by overseers and masters. In short, slaves were considered property—with no legal rights or freedoms.

Within the confines of the slavery system, African Americans developed a unique culture. Most slaves had come from West African countries—modern-day Senegal, Gambia, Ghana, and Gabon. Their culture was derived from the traditions of these regions, mixed with American and European elements. West African religions became fused with and dominated by Christianity. Forbidden to speak their native languages, slaves developed a kind of pidgin (simplified) English. Drumming, the dominant form of music in West Africa, was also banned, as masters believed drumming to be a method of communication, perhaps a way for slaves to organize a rebellion. Singing was permitted, though. Through religious and secular songs, slaves often sang of freedom and escape to the North.

A traditional slave dance in New Orleans

A drummer boy for the all-black 78th regiment. Many black men joined the Union army during the Civil War.

3
SLAVERY SPLITS THE NATION

By the early 19th century, slavery had become a controversial issue in the United States—dividing the nation, North and South. Southern slave owners believed their plantations couldn't profit without slave labor. They also wanted to permit slavery in the new states joining the quickly expanding Union. Abolitionists, based mainly in the North, were people who opposed slavery. They wanted to eliminate slavery in the United States altogether or at least limit the practice to those areas in which it already existed.

Many abolitionists condemned slavery as an evil practice—against God's law. A number of church groups lent their support to the abolitionist cause. Other abolitionists were European immigrants who had fled oppression in Europe and opposed slavery or serfdom in any form.

Not all Northerners were opposed to slavery. Poor whites feared that freed blacks would compete with them for jobs and drive down wages. Some whites opposed slavery on ethical grounds, but still felt that blacks were inferior to whites and not deserving of full rights and privileges.

Although they were technically free, blacks in most northern states were denied basic rights, such as the right to vote. They worked menial, low-paying jobs. And freed or escaped slaves were under the constant threat of being captured and taken back into slavery.

Determined to keep blacks from power, and fearing that free blacks might lead slaves in revolt, several white politicians formed the American Colonization Society

In the North, the abolition movement was becoming stronger and more vocal.

in 1816. This group essentially wanted to rid the United States of its black population, and it encouraged the voluntary migration of blacks to Africa. Only about 12,000 blacks made the trip, however, eventually establishing the nation of Liberia in West Africa.

Although most African Americans were farmhands in the mid-1800s, some lived and worked in cities. These men are dockworkers.

Follow the North Star

While the slavery debate raged, African Americans made attempts to free themselves. Since slaves were closely watched by their overseers and were usually scattered among distant plantations, large-scale organizing was difficult. Denmark Vesey in 1822 and Nat Turner in 1831 tried to lead groups of slaves in revolt—Vesey in South Carolina; Turner in Virginia. Both uprisings were put down and their leaders hanged.

Other slaves tried to escape. Between about 1830 and

1860, thousands made their way north through a secret abolitionist network known as the Underground Railroad. Runaway slaves traveled at night and hid during the day, assisted by both black and white guides. One such guide was Harriet Tubman, a former slave who went south and helped more than 300 runaways. Because escaped slaves could be captured in northern states and returned to slavery under U.S. law, many fugitives went to Canada.

Tubman and several other former slaves became famous abolitionists. Sojourner Truth, born in New York in 1797, preached throughout the country about both abolition and women's rights. Frederick Douglass, born in Maryland in 1817, lectured against slavery in the United States and Great Britain. He founded a weekly antislavery newspaper, the *North Star*, in 1847.

Political Turmoil

Trying to keep the slavery debate from boiling over into war, Congress passed the Missouri Compromise in 1820. This plan allowed the Union to admit one slave state for every free state admitted, so that no one side could outvote the other in the Senate. The compromise worked reasonably well until 1850, when California asked to be admitted as a free state, and no slave area was available to match it.

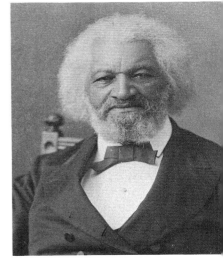

Frederick Douglass

By this time, the North and South were far apart on the slavery issue. Southern leaders wanted to make slavery legal throughout the United States. While in the North, the abolition movement was becoming stronger and more vocal.

The last attempt at compromise came with the Kansas-Nebraska Act of 1854. This law granted territorial citizens the right to vote for or against slavery before their region joined the Union as a state. The result was "Bleeding Kansas," where pro- and antislavery forces fought one another, each side trying to bring in the most settlers. Eventually, Kansas was admitted to the Union as a free state.

The year 1854 also saw the creation of the Republican Party, which took a strong stance against slavery. The Republican presidential candidate did well in the 1856 election, although Democrat James Buchanan won the office. Southerners feared the Republican Party's power, though. If a Republican president were ever elected, southern leaders declared, the South would secede, or withdraw from the United States.

Proslavery forces won a significant victory with the Dred Scott decision in 1857. Scott was a slave who sued for his freedom on the grounds that he had once lived on free soil. The Supreme Court denied his claim, declaring that slaves were property; they could be bought, sold, or traded. Under this ruling, a slave owner could take his property anywhere—even to a free state—as he desired. The Court also said that blacks could not become U.S. citizens. Northerners grew more fearful that slavery would spread. Many joined the Republican Party.

Freedom would not be easy.

The Nation at War

In 1860 Republican Abraham Lincoln was elected president of the United States. South Carolina was the first southern state to make good on its threat to secede after Lincoln's victory. Ten more states soon followed. They formed the Confederate States of America and elected Jefferson Davis as their president. The federal government vowed to use force to bring the rebellious states back into the Union. The country was at war.

African Americans participated in the Civil War in large numbers. More than 200,000 black men served in the Union army and navy. About 40,000 died in battle and another 20,000 died of disease during their military service.

But despite their achievements in combat, black soldiers encountered great prejudice. Many northern soldiers felt they were not fighting against slavery at all, but rather to preserve the Union. They greeted black soldiers with hostility and derision. Blacks were paid less than whites and were assigned to segregated units.

The Veteran, *painted in 1866 by Thomas Waterman Wood*

Eventually, some black soldiers were given commissions as officers. But very few ever commanded a large number of troops.

As Union troops pushed into the South, they found runaway slaves and weren't sure how to treat them. Since African Americans were not citizens, but "property," they were at first returned to their masters. Finally, they were declared "contraband of war" and sent north. Some runaway slaves joined the Union army.

But what of the nearly four million African Americans who remained enslaved in the South? By 1862 Lincoln knew he had to take a firm stand on slavery. The abolitionists were strong. They had voted for him, and they wanted action.

On January 1, 1863, Lincoln issued the Emancipation Proclamation, declaring that slaves in areas of rebellion against the United States were forever free. Blacks rejoiced throughout the nation. The proclamation was more a symbolic action than a law, though, since slavery was not officially abolished until 1865, with the passage of the 13th Amendment to the U.S. Constitution.

The Civil War ended with the Confederate surrender at Appomattox Court House, Virginia, in April 1865. The end of the war and the end of slavery meant a new way of life for the Africans in America. But freedom would not be easy. The South lay in ruins. Thousands of Southerners had lost their homes, families, and livelihoods

Runaway slaves at a Maryland farm, 1862

during the war. Southern blacks faced a particularly uncertain future. They were no longer slaves, but not yet citizens. Most African Americans had no money, job skills, or land. Some, knowing no other life, even wanted to stay with their masters after the war.

To restore national unity, the federal government set out to rebuild the South and to bring the Confederate states back into the Union. This period of redevelopment, known as Reconstruction, lasted until 1877. It was far from peaceful. Many Northerners abused the Reconstruction system for their own financial or political gain. White Southerners resented and resisted northern control. Black Americans were once again caught in the middle of a passionate debate.

A scene envisioned by a 19th-century painter: A Union soldier reads the Emancipation Proclamation to a black family.

Household workers on a South Carolina estate, 1899. Many African Americans continued to work for white landowners after the Civil War.

4
A FRAGILE FREEDOM

The federal government's original Reconstruction plan stated that if 10 percent of the voters in any seceded state would take an oath of allegiance to the United States and agree to abide by federal policies on slavery, then that state would be readmitted to the Union. It could organize a state government, send representatives to Congress, and resume its place among the United States.

But a number of Congress members, known as the Radical Republicans, wanted to punish the South for its rebellion. The 10 percent plan was too lenient, they said. The Radicals wanted to give black men the right to vote and wanted to keep white Southerners out of Congress and other branches of government.

President Andrew Johnson, who took office upon Abraham Lincoln's assassination in 1865, opposed the Radicals. He offered pardons to all but the most prominent Confederate leaders and encouraged the South's quick readmission to the Union. But the Radicals were a strong force in Congress. After much debate, they prevailed.

Two amendments were quickly added to the Constitution. The 14th Amendment, ratified in 1868, made black people citizens of the United States and barred former Confederate leaders from holding state and federal office. The 15th Amendment, ratified in 1870, gave black men the right to vote. Southern states had to ratify these two amendments before being readmitted to the Union, and federal troops were stationed throughout the South to enforce the new laws.

Black Americans were now citizens, and black men were voters. To ensure Republican control in the South,

African-American children, late 19th century

29

northern politicians encouraged blacks to vote and backed black candidates in local, state, and national elections. Several black men won seats in the South Carolina legislature. Pinckney Pinchback became acting governor of Louisiana, and Blanche Bruce represented Mississippi in the United States Senate. Other blacks were elected to the House of Representatives.

A federal agency known as the Freedmen's Bureau set out to improve the lives of black Americans in other ways. In operation between 1865 and 1872, the bureau set up hospitals, provided job training, and helped blacks buy land. It established black colleges, such as Atlanta University, Howard University, Hampton Institute, and Fisk, and set up thousands of elementary and secondary schools for black children.

Black leaders were determined to carry their community forward.

White Terror

All these changes did not sit well with white Southerners. They resented northern control and detested the notion of former slaves holding political office. As federal troops began to withdraw and as time passed after Reconstruction, whites once again took control in the South. White voters ousted blacks from positions of power and influence. They also began a campaign of terror against black Americans.

Throughout the South, white supremacist groups such as the Ku Klux Klan burned, beat, and lynched blacks at will. White people who tried to help blacks were also terrorized. KKK members wore ghostly white sheets and hoods and burned crosses to advertise their meetings or give warnings. The organization grew quickly. Many county and state officials were Klan members.

The white supremacist movement also brought about "black codes," laws meant to deny rights to African Americans. In many parts of the South, blacks were not allowed to testify in court against a white person. They could not own firearms. In some areas, black people could not own the land on which they lived.

White Southerners also devised ways to deny blacks

the right to vote. Southern officials often imposed a special tax on voters, called a poll tax, which most blacks could not afford. In other cases, blacks were asked to read and explain parts of the federal or state constitution before voting. Many blacks had no education; they were turned away from the polls because they couldn't read. Other blacks were denied membership in political parties and kept from voting in party elections.

Further denial of rights came by segregating (separating) blacks from whites in public places such as schools, theaters, rest rooms, dining halls, and trains. Almost without exception, facilities set aside for black Americans were inferior to those provided for whites. Systems of segregation and discrimination against blacks came to be called Jim Crow laws, or simply Jim Crow, named after a black minstrel character of the mid-19th century.

In the decades after the war, most blacks continued to do farmwork, but did not own their own land.

A Struggle to Survive

Without money to buy land, most black Southerners farmed someone else's property. They were known as tenant farmers, or sharecroppers. Usually in debt to their landlords, tenant families lived under a system not much better than the slave life they had left behind. Their farmland was poor, rent was high, and they were underpaid for their crops. By the 1870s, conditions for tenant farmers had become desperate. Drought and disease damaged crops and forced sharecroppers deeper into debt.

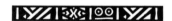

African Americans arrived in cities like Chicago full of hope for a better future.

In 1879 some southern blacks began an exodus to Kansas and the West—hoping to find better jobs and less racial prejudice there. The number of people who left was fairly small, probably not more than 30,000. Some black leaders opposed the move. They said the migration would scatter the black community and reduce what little power it had. Furthermore, many blacks feared that they would not be received with open arms in the West, Kansas, or the North. In the end, they were often correct.

The North was no promised land for blacks. Although the abolition movement had flourished there, Jim Crow flourished there as well. Some northern officials devised schemes to deny voting rights to blacks. Many states passed laws against intermarriage and mixed-race athletic events. Schools, housing, and railroad facilities were often segregated—if not by law then by practice.

Blacks who went north usually had no choice but to take the lowest paying and most menial jobs. When hard times came, black workers were the first to lose their positions. Many blacks who went north returned to the South in despair.

Poised for Change

By 1910, nearly 50 years after the Civil War, more than 85 percent of the African-American population still lived in the South. Most were sharecroppers, but about

25 percent owned their own land. Their holdings were not as large or as fertile as those owned by white farmers. But the black community had made some important gains. In 1880 only about 30 percent of the black population could read and write. By 1910 almost 70 percent were literate. Life expectancy had increased slightly for black people, and more were employed. Still, black Americans had not achieved equal rights, and many were desperately poor.

Black leaders were determined to carry their community forward. Some leaders felt the most pressing needs of their people were education, jobs, and technical skills. One such man was Booker T. Washington, who founded Tuskegee Institute in Alabama—one of the most prominent black colleges in the nation. Washington

Booker T. Washington

Students at Tuskegee Institute in Alabama

believed that black people should focus on education and employment. Equal rights would follow, he argued, after blacks had attended to their basic economic needs.

Harvard-educated W. E. B. Du Bois differed with Washington. To Du Bois, Washington was a compromiser—willing to let blacks settle for second-place status in American society. Du Bois believed that blacks needed to speak out strongly against racial discrimination. He urged the most talented African Americans to take leadership roles in politics, education, and business. In 1909 Du Bois and other black leaders formed the National Association for the Advancement of Colored People (NAACP) in New York state. It would become one of the most powerful civil rights groups of the 20th century. As the new century dawned, the Africans in America were poised for action.

W. E. B. Du Bois

5
THE ROAD NORTH

When World War I began in Europe in 1914, American industry geared up to produce the tools of war—tanks, airplanes, guns, and battleships. There were jobs to be had in the foundries and factories of northern industrial cities—but these jobs usually went to white men.

At first the United States sent only supplies and equipment to its allies fighting in Europe. But by 1917, the United States had officially entered the war. Thousands of working men joined the armed forces, and their jobs at home had to be filled. Blacks needed work and the defense industry supplied it. Thus began a mass migration north.

About 500,000 African Americans moved north during World War I. They took trains to Pittsburgh, Cleveland, Detroit, New York, St. Louis, and other big cities. Around 100,000 black people moved to Chicago—where the stockyards alone offered thousands of jobs. Others went west, seeking defense industry work in Los Angeles. The NAACP and the National Urban League played an important role in the migration. These groups helped locate work for the new arrivals and tried to find them decent housing in industrial cities.

Broken Promises

African Americans arrived in cities like Chicago full of hope for a better future. But these hopes were quickly dashed. Many black men were told that they did not have the skills necessary for factory work. They had to take lower paying jobs as janitors, dishwashers, and trash haulers. Black women worked as maids and cooks. Even those black people lucky enough to secure jobs in industry struggled with prejudice. Labor unions did not usually accept black members. So black workers were denied the economic benefits and protection that unions could provide. Blacks usually received lower wages than whites, even for the same job, and there was little hope for blacks to move into supervisory positions, particularly when the jobs involved supervising white workers.

Glass factory workers near Washington, D.C., 1911

Mississippi children

Segregation and high rents combined to keep blacks from decent housing too. So the newcomers concentrated in poor inner-city neighborhoods. Hardly welcomed by white Northerners, blacks found that many stores, theaters, and restaurants wouldn't serve them. Tension built in the inner cities and several times boiled over into riots.

Democracy for Some

A few black leaders thought that African Americans shouldn't support the war effort. They argued that democracy should be secured at home—for black citizens—instead of on some distant European battlefield. The overwhelming majority of blacks, however, supported the American effort during World War I. Almost 2,300,000 black men registered for the draft, and some 367,000 were called for military duty.

A social club for black
soldiers, World War I

Almost all black men served in segregated units. They faced prejudice not only from white troops and officers but also from white civilians near military training camps. Fighting broke out between blacks and whites near military bases in Houston, Texas; Spartanburg, South Carolina; and other towns during the war.

About 200,000 black soldiers served in Europe. One all-black unit, the 369th Infantry from New York, spent 191 days in combat in 1918. It was the first Allied unit to reach the Rhine River. More than 170 of its officers and enlisted men were decorated by the French government for their achievements in battle.

When the war ended, some black soldiers wondered if they should return home from Europe. After all, the French had treated them with dignity. The United States offered only racial prejudice. A few black veterans did stay in Europe, while the majority came home to their towns and families. But rather than thank returning black soldiers, the nation treated them with distrust. Some white leaders claimed that black soldiers had been exposed to "foreign political ideas" in Europe and that they could not be trusted as loyal Americans.

In addition, white men returning from war wanted their jobs back. Many black workers were fired at war's end. And the Ku Klux Klan was back at work, stirring up hatred toward Jews, Catholics, and other minority groups—especially blacks. By the end of World War I, the Klan operated in more than 30 states. Blacks were lynched, terrorized, and kept from the polls.

Indiana Klan members, early 20th century

By 1921 the United States was in a slight economic depression. The black community was hit especially hard—as blacks were the first to lose their jobs when businesses made cutbacks. Although life was hard in northern cities, blacks continued to migrate there from the South, looking for work, hoping for a better life. Between 1910 and 1930, one million black Americans moved north.

Alain Locke

An American Renaissance

There were some gains for African Americans after the war. In the 1920s, the automobile and tobacco industries began hiring more black workers. Some African Americans found jobs in the textile industry, operating largely in southern cities. Almost all railroad firefighters and porters were black men, and they built a powerful union, the Brotherhood of Sleeping Car Porters, led by A. Philip Randolph.

Harlem, New York, during this period, was the site of an era of creative expression known as the Harlem Renaissance. Writers Langston Hughes, Alain Locke, Dorothy West, and others fueled the Harlem cultural

Oystermen in Virginia

Marcus Garvey

scene. Across the nation, the black press took on an expanded role. Newspapers like the *Chicago Weekly Defender,* the *Pittsburgh Courier,* the *California Eagle,* and the *Amsterdam News* allowed African Americans to voice their hopes and concerns. At the same time, black colleges provided an education to those fortunate enough to gain admittance. Largely barred from white colleges and universities, black students enrolled at Tuskegee Institute, Fisk University in Nashville, Central State in Ohio, and Morehouse in Atlanta.

Many black Americans of the 1920s joined the Universal Negro Improvement Association, led by Marcus Garvey. Jamaican-born Garvey believed that blacks would never receive justice from the white majority in the United States, and he argued that blacks should return to their African homeland. An estimated two million Americans joined his cause. Although Garvey's plans for an African homeland were never realized, he was instrumental in building black businesses in the United States and promoting racial pride.

6
THE DOORS BEGIN TO OPEN

In 1929 the United States entered the Great Depression. By 1932 millions of Americans were out of work. Many stood in line at soup kitchens. Banks and businesses closed. Most African Americans were poor. Now the situation was worse.

A former slave, Cudjo Lewis, and his great-grandchildren in Mobile, Alabama, 1927

The election of 1932 brought Democrat Franklin D. Roosevelt to the White House, and with him a greatly expanded program of government action. Through this program, known as the New Deal, Roosevelt established agencies to help the unemployed, bolster the economy, and put industry back to work.

The Roosevelt administration was one place in the United States where barriers of race and color were finally lowered. Prior to Roosevelt's election, civil service (government) jobseekers had been required to state their race or color and submit a picture with their job applications. Roosevelt stopped this practice. He made efforts to equalize wages and forbid discrimination in hiring for government jobs. Thousands of black Americans found work as clerks, typists, and administrators in Roosevelt's New Deal agencies. The federal government soon became the largest employer of blacks in the nation.

African Americans had an ally in the president's cabinet, namely Harold Ickes, secretary of the interior. Ickes, a former president of the Chicago NAACP, hired many African Americans onto his staff. Eleanor Roosevelt, the president's wife, was a strong champion of racial justice.

The president also gathered advice on minority affairs from a group of African-American leaders known as the Black Cabinet. These consultants were experts in their various professions, and they represented a new generation of black Americans entering public service. One of the president's most respected consultants was Walter White, longtime head of the NAACP. His influence helped open many doors to blacks in the New Deal period. Among other black newcomers to federal office were Robert C. Weaver, Ralph Bunche, and Mary McLeod Bethune. The employment of these people in powerful positions gave black America hope that many others would soon follow.

The policies of the New Deal also brought blacks into the Democratic Party in large numbers. Since the Civil War, blacks had tended to vote Republican—the party of Lincoln, the Great Emancipator. To many blacks, the

Mary McLeod Bethune served in various government and educational positions. She advised President Roosevelt, founded the National Council for Negro Women, and founded Bethune-Cookman College, an all-black school in Daytona Beach, Florida.

Adam Clayton Powell Jr.

Democratic Party stood for oppression, white suprema-
cists, and southern influence. As the years went by,
however, blacks began to doubt the Republican Party's
commitment to black citizens. This doubt grew in the
1920s, as Republicans tried to appeal to white voters
in the South and did very little for black Americans.
By 1936 most blacks were voting Democratic—the party
of Roosevelt.

Blacks also began to run for office on the Democratic
ticket. In 1934 Arthur Mitchell of Chicago became the
first black Democrat ever elected to Congress. He defeated incumbent Oscar De Priest, a Republican and
the first black person elected to Congress in the 20th
century.

Adam Clayton Powell Sr., a prominent New York City
minister, joined the Democratic Party in 1936. A leading
enemy of corruption in city government, his influence
helped put his son, Adam Powell Jr., into Congress.

During Powell's 24 years as a representative, he authored more than 50 pieces of legislation, promoting civil rights, job training, education, integration, and other social programs.

Once More to War

The United States entered World War II in December 1941, after the Japanese attack on Pearl Harbor, Hawaii. Within days, the United States was officially at war with Japan and its allies, Germany and Italy. As they had during World War I, some black leaders asked why blacks should fight for democracy elsewhere when they did not freely enjoy it in the United States. But most African Americans supported the war effort.

Black people had a few reasons of their own to want to fight—specifically with Italy and Germany. They had been distressed by Italy's conquest of Ethiopia a few years earlier. Some African Americans had even joined the Ethiopian military. Blacks also feared German dictator Adolf Hitler and his ideas about the supremacy of Aryan (northern European) people. The black community had despaired when German boxer Max Schmeling defeated the black hero Joe Louis in 1936. When Louis made a brilliant comeback against Schmeling in 1938, African Americans were overjoyed.

In 1940, when the military draft began, the U.S. government announced that blacks would be taken into the armed services in proportion to their numbers in the total population (about 10 percent). In all, more than 3,000,000 black men registered for the draft. More than 700,000 served in the army, about 165,000 in the navy, 17,000 in the Marine Corps, and 5,000 in the Coast Guard. Almost 500,000 served overseas.

Black soldiers still served in segregated units, though, and were commanded largely by white officers. The military rarely gave blacks positions of responsibility, instead assigning them to construction work, the recovery of dead bodies, and other noncombat jobs. When black leaders protested, the government put black

Joe Louis

Naval recruits, 1943

and white leaders to work on plans to improve the status of blacks in the armed services. One immediate result of the protest was the appointment of a few blacks to high positions. Benjamin O. Davis Sr. was promoted to brigadier general—the first black person to reach this rank. Judge William Hastie was named civilian aide to the secretary of war. But Hastie thought the government wasn't doing enough to end discrimination in the military. He resigned his position in protest in 1943.

By war's end, thousands of black soldiers had been commissioned as officers. Black women had joined the various women's military units such as the WACS and

WAVES. Most branches of the military had integrated their officer candidate schools. Some integration took place in special or selected army units on an experimental basis. But there still had been no military-wide integration.

Home Front Blues

Conditions at home during World War II were much the same as they had been 30 years before. As white men went into military service, jobs opened up throughout the country. Thousands of black people poured into cities like Detroit and Los Angeles and found jobs in defense plants and other industries. For the first time, black women were also employed in defense work and manufacturing.

But the obstacles had not changed much since 1917 either. Unions were usually closed to blacks. The best jobs were often taken by whites, and wages for blacks were lower than those of their white counterparts. In addition, housing for black defense workers was scarce, overpriced, and usually segregated and substandard.

But African Americans were no longer going to accept these conditions quietly. Soon after the United States entered the war, labor leader A. Philip Randolph threatened a mass march on Washington, D.C., to protest discrimination in the defense industry. Under pressure from Randolph and other black leaders, on June 25, 1941, President Roosevelt issued Executive Order 8802, stating that "there shall be no discrimination in the employment of workers in defense industries or Government because of race, creed, color, or national origin." Defense contracts from then on were written to comply with the order, and a federal commission was set up to investigate violations and complaints. Executive Order 8802 applied only to defense industries and thus did not address discrimination in the rest of American employment. But it was a first step—one that enabled many African Americans to get better jobs and treatment.

A. Philip Randolph

47

World War II ended in September 1945. Defense plants closed, soldiers returned home, and once again many black Americans lost their jobs to white veterans. But the U.S. economy prospered. Employment levels stayed high, and African Americans benefitted from both the prosperity and further government action. First, President Harry S. Truman issued an executive order making fair employment guarantees a part of most contracts between government and private industry. Then, in 1948, Truman issued Executive Order 9981, calling for integration of the armed forces and equal treatment of all military personnel. During the Korean War, between 1950 and 1953, integrated army units served with distinction, and two black Americans were awarded Congressional Medals of Honor for bravery.

New jobs opened for black women during World War II. These women worked for the B & O railroad.

The color barrier also began to fall in sports and the arts. In 1947 Jackie Robinson became the first black player in major-league baseball, setting the stage for the integration of all professional sports. Black musicians—Louis Armstrong, Duke Ellington, Billie Holiday, and many others—had become popular among white as well as black audiences. Musical styles like jazz and rhythm and blues, rooted in African-American tradition, were setting the standard for the entire music industry. By the mid-1950s, writers like Richard Wright, Gwendolyn Brooks, and James Baldwin were bringing the African-American experience to the book-buying public.

But despite these advancements, Jim Crow remained strong. In many states, voting rights were still denied to blacks. Education, housing, and employment opportunities were restricted. And, particularly in the South, racism and legalized segregation combined to keep blacks from achieving full equality.

Gwendolyn Brooks won several literary awards, including the 1950 Pulitzer Prize for poetry.

In the middle decades of the 20th century, Louis Armstrong was America's premier jazz musician and bandleader.

March on Washington for civil rights, August 1963

7
UNFINISHED BUSINESS

After World War II, the struggle to secure the legal rights of black people moved to the nation's courts. There, blacks began to see significant victories. In 1944 the Supreme Court decreed that black voters could not be prevented from participating in primary elections. In 1946 a Virginia law requiring segregation on interstate buses was declared to be invalid. Two years later, the Supreme Court ruled that restrictive covenants—private agreements to prevent members of minority groups from buying property—could not be enforced by federal or state courts.

Such legal rulings were significant, but the most important court decisions were those related to education. At the end of the 19th century, the Supreme Court, in the case of *Plessy v. Ferguson,* had established the "separate but equal" principle as a justification for segregation. Public facilities such as schools could be segregated, the Court had ruled, as long facilities for blacks were equal to those used by whites.

But black schools were seldom equal to white schools in any sense of the word. Schoolbooks—if there were enough to go around—were often secondhand and out of date. Schoolhouses for black children were crowded and run-down. Black teachers were paid less than white teachers.

As early as the 1930s, the NAACP began to bring test cases before the Supreme Court in an effort to challenge the separate but equal doctrine. In 1938 the University of Missouri was forced to admit a black student to its law school, because there was no equal black school available to him. Similar decisions were made in Oklahoma in 1948 and in Texas in 1950.

Enforcing court decisions was slow and difficult work.

The struggle against the separate but equal principle reached a climax in 1954, when the case of *Brown v. the Board of Education of Topeka* reached the Supreme Court. The suit had been filed on behalf of Linda Brown, a black schoolchild barred from attending an all-white school near her home in Topeka, Kansas. In the case, Thurgood Marshall, then chief legal counsel for the NAACP, argued that the separate but equal doctrine was invalid, because separate schools were by their very nature unequal. The court agreed and ruled that enforced segregation in public schools was unconstitutional. This ruling in effect overturned the earlier *Plessy v. Ferguson* decision.

Thurgood Marshall

The school desegregation ruling had tremendous impact not only on the American educational system but also on many other areas of American life. If enforced segregation in the schools was unconstitutional, black

"Colored Only" and "White Only" were once common signs on storefronts, water fountains, public rest rooms, and buses in the American South.

leaders argued, then the same principle should apply to other segregated facilities, like restaurants, theaters, and bus stations. Many communities, faced with court action, did away with restrictions and laws that had existed for 100 years. The desegregation ruling had its most profound effects in the schools, though. In 1955 the Supreme Court ordered that integration in the public schools should take place "with all deliberate speed." During the following years, partial desegregation was accomplished peacefully in hundreds of schools throughout the nation.

But some communities would not comply with the Court's ruling. In parts of the South, business and civic leaders organized White Citizens Councils to defend segregation to the end. The Ku Klux Klan underwent another revival. Black parents who tried to enroll their children in "white schools" were fired from their jobs, refused credit at banks, evicted from their homes, and attacked physically.

Violence broke out in Little Rock, Arkansas, in 1957, when school officials attempted to integrate Little Rock Central High School. Despite the federal court order,

Federal troops escort black students into Central High School in Little Rock.

Inside a Birmingham, Alabama, bus

the governor of Arkansas sent the National Guard to prevent black students from entering the school. Token integration of Central High occurred only after President Dwight Eisenhower ordered federal troops into Little Rock.

Trying New Tactics

Enforcing court decisions was slow and difficult work. The NAACP, under the leadership of Roy Wilkins, continued to bring civil rights cases to court, but many black people became impatient with the legal process. They were also discouraged by the violent reactions of whites to desegregation efforts.

In 1955 blacks in Montgomery, Alabama, decided to take a new approach. Led by Baptist minister Martin Luther King Jr., they organized a boycott to protest segregated seating on city buses. The boycott began after the arrest of Rosa Parks, a civil rights activist who refused to give up her seat to a white man on a

Martin Luther King Jr.

crowded Montgomery bus. For 382 days, Montgomery's black citizens carpooled or walked to and from work rather than support the city bus system. As a result of this protest, the city of Montgomery abolished its segregated seating law.

With the success of the Montgomery boycott, other black leaders began using boycotts and demonstrations to protest unjust laws and to demand equal treatment. Young black people organized "sit-ins" at segregated lunch counters throughout the South. "Wade-ins" were held at segregated beaches and "pray-ins" at all-white churches. During the summer of 1961, blacks and sympathetic whites boarded buses and made "Freedom Rides" to protest segregation in bus stations and on public transportation.

Martin Luther King believed in the philosophy of nonviolent resistance and urged his followers to adopt nonviolent methods in their struggle. Protesters learned

Roy Wilkins

A "sit-in" at a segregated Arkansas lunch counter

how to control their tempers under all circumstances and how to protect themselves from physical abuse without striking back. Civil rights demonstrations, now seen on television, caught the nation's attention. Many Americans were impressed by the peaceful manner in which the young protesters conducted their marches and sit-ins. Many Northerners, particularly white college students, were drawn to the civil rights cause.

Three groups took the lead in the struggle: the Southern Christian Leadership Conference (SCLC), founded in 1957 by King and other black clergymen, the Congress of Racial Equality (CORE), and the Student Nonviolent Coordinating Committee (SNCC). By the early 1960s, results began to show, as businesses throughout the South quietly desegregated their facilities rather than face the unfavorable publicity of a sit-in or demonstration.

The year 1963 marked a high point of civil rights activities. Leaders organized nonviolent demonstrations all over the South, protesting segregation and voting rights restrictions. In Birmingham, Alabama, police turned attack dogs and high-pressure fire hoses on the demonstrators. Many protesters, including Martin Luther King, were jailed. News footage of the events in Birmingham shocked the American public and the world.

A police dog attacks a demonstrator in Birmingham, Alabama, May 1963.

In August of that year, more than 200,000 people took part in a march on Washington, D.C., as an expression of solidarity and concern for civil rights. The march was led by a multiracial group, including A. Philip Randolph, Urban League chief Whitney Young Jr., NAACP head Roy Wilkins, and others. The highlight of the march was Martin Luther King's "I Have a Dream" speech, delivered at the base of the Lincoln Memorial. In this famous speech, Dr. King spoke eloquently about judging people by the content of their character, not by the color of their skin.

While King and other civil rights leaders were working toward racial integration, other black groups were urging separation of the races. The Nation of Islam, founded in 1930, became increasingly influential in the 1960s. The group's leader, Elijah Muhammad, believed

Malcolm X

that conflict between blacks and whites was inevitable, and he prepared his followers to meet violence with violence. The Nation of Islam hoped to eventually establish a separate black nation within the United States.

The most popular black nationalist was Malcolm X, a fiery speaker who attracted many urban blacks to the nationalist cause. In 1964, after a disagreement with Elijah Muhammad, Malcolm X left the Nation of Islam and formed a rival nationalist group. The following year, he was assassinated. Nation of Islam members were convicted of the crime.

In the nation's capital, the federal government could no longer ignore the struggle. In 1957 Congress set up a commission on civil rights—the first federal civil rights action since Reconstruction—to investigate civil

rights violations. Another federal law, designed to protect the voting rights of blacks, was enacted in 1960.

In 1963, when widespread protest demonstrations had captured the nation's attention, a comprehensive civil rights bill finally reached Congress. Initiated by President John F. Kennedy, the bill outlawed discrimination in restaurants, hotels, and other public places. It forbade discrimination by employers and unions and established a commission to enforce fair employment practices. It withheld federal funds from any program or activity that allowed racial discrimination.

In November 1963, President Kennedy was assassinated. The civil rights bill was still in Congress, and Kennedy's successor, Lyndon B. Johnson, urged that it be passed quickly. In July 1964, the bill became law.

President Lyndon Johnson meets with Martin Luther King Jr. (third from left) and other black leaders at the White House.

White Backlash

In 1964 Martin Luther King was awarded the Nobel Peace Prize. His philosophy of nonviolence had served the cause of civil rights well. But many black people were disturbed that nonviolent protest often brought a violent response. In much of the South, blacks were still terrorized by the KKK and intimidated at the polls. In 1964 three young civil rights workers were murdered during a voter registration drive in Mississippi. Bombs were placed in black churches and meeting halls. Between 1960 and 1965, more than 30 civil rights activists were killed.

In January 1965, King began a voting rights campaign centered in Selma, Alabama. During the tense two-month-long drive, four people were killed, and many more who attempted to register voters were threatened or arrested. When demonstrators tried to march from Selma to the state capitol in Montgomery, they were stopped by police officers using tear gas and whips. Hundreds of sympathizers, black and white, rushed to Selma to join the march. Finally, President Johnson ordered federal protection for the demonstrators, who made the walk from Selma to Montgomery in late March.

White men taunt civil rights marchers in Selma, Alabama. National Guardsmen, sent to protect marchers from violence, look on.

59

In August 1965, with Selma still in the news and on the mind of the nation, Congress passed the Voting Rights Act, outlawing literacy tests for voters and permitting federal examiners to supervise voter registration. The next year, the Supreme Court ruled that local and state poll taxes were illegal. (In 1964, the 24th Amendment to the U.S. Constitution had prohibited poll taxes in federal elections.) As a result of these measures, the number of black voters in the South rose dramatically, as did the election of blacks to public office.

Urban Uprising

Although civil rights protests were centered in the South, by the mid-1960s almost half of America's black population lived in large metropolitan areas in the North. Many others lived in the West, specifically in Los Angeles.

Floyd McKissick of CORE

A lot of white Americans thought of racial discrimination as a southern problem. The blacks of America's big industrial cities—living in ghettos and plagued by unemployment—knew otherwise. Civil rights legislation had not been able to give African Americans jobs or provide better schools for their children. It did not do away with slums, nor did it prevent the discriminatory practices that kept black people out of decent housing. Racial discrimination in the North and West was sometimes more subtle than it was in the South, but it was a reality. Racial tension brewed under the surface in big American cities.

Tension turned into violence in August 1965, when a confrontation between black citizens and white police officers set off a riot in the Watts area of Los Angeles. The rioting lasted for five days. More than 30 people were killed, and hundreds of businesses were looted and burned. The stores of white merchants were special targets of the rioters, while most black-owned businesses were spared.

Meanwhile, fueled by victories in the South, the NAACP, CORE, SNCC, and other civil rights groups moved their fight north. In 1966 Martin Luther King led open-housing marches to protest racial segregation in Chicago's white neighborhoods. Angry whites threw rocks at the marchers.

In Detroit violence was met with violence. In July 1967, riots erupted in Detroit's black ghetto—again set off by a confrontation between black citizens and the police. The disturbance lasted a week and took 43 lives. Buildings were burned, and thousands of Detroiters were left homeless. Federal troops using tanks, armored cars, and machine guns finally put an end to the riot.

Afterward, President Johnson appointed a commission to study the causes of urban rioting and to recommend ways of preventing further disturbances. The commission, headed by Illinois governor Otto Kerner, presented its findings in March 1968. The report stated that racism and discrimination were the underlying

Children play in front of the Robert Taylor Homes, a public housing project in inner-city Chicago.

causes of the riots. The commission warned that more unrest would follow and that the nation would become increasingly divided unless black people were allowed to assume an equal place with whites in American society.

Black Power

In 1966 Stokely Carmichael, a young black activist born in the West Indies, was elected chairman of SNCC. Carmichael believed that African Americans needed to take a new approach in their struggle for equality. Instead of seeking integration into white society, he argued, blacks should develop their own institutions and preserve their own unique culture. They should work to elect black politicians. They should start their own businesses. Carmichael's ideas formed the basis of the Black Power movement.

SNCC enthusiastically endorsed Black Power, as did CORE, under the leadership of Floyd McKissick. But more traditional civil rights groups, the NAACP and SCLC, were at first opposed to the new ideas. The advocates of Black Power did not believe in nonviolence; they wanted black people to defend themselves against attack and to be aggressive in fighting for their rights. Some black leaders were also disturbed by Black Power policies calling for the withdrawal of white volunteers from civil rights organizations.

Despite initial disagreements, the Black Power movement eventually won widespread support—even among traditional civil rights leaders. By urging blacks to find solutions to their own problems, the movement promoted self-respect and self-confidence. It encouraged African Americans to take pride in their skin color, in their customs, in everything that made them unique and different from the white majority. African-American music, literature, and art of the late 1960s reflected this sense of pride. Even athletes—boxer Muhammad Ali and Olympic track athletes Tommie Smith and John Carlos—promoted Black Power from the victory stand.

A new generation of black leaders was emerging on the political scene.

Perhaps the most extreme segment of the Black Power movement was the Black Panther Party. Founded in 1966 by Huey Newton and Bobby Seale, the organization called for a revolutionary change in the economic and political structure of American society—a change to be brought about by violence if necessary. Local Black Panther groups armed themselves in self-defense. Police raids on Panther headquarters sometimes resulted in fatal gun battles.

The Black Panthers were few in number, but their voices were loud and their words inflammatory. Many white Americans were frightened by the Panthers. But many African Americans approved of the group. The Panthers projected an image of defiance and strength, of racial pride and courage. Black pride was growing, and more gains appeared to be just around the corner.

Children and adults give the Black Power salute, 1969.

Then, in April 1968, Martin Luther King—in Memphis, Tennessee, to support striking sanitation workers—was assassinated by a hidden gunman. The black community was stunned and outraged. Rioting occurred in black communities throughout the nation.

At the time of the assassination, a new civil rights bill was stalled in the House of Representatives. The measure primarily addressed housing discrimination, but also dealt with equal employment opportunities and protection of civil rights workers. Fearing even more violence in America's cities, the House quickly passed the bill. Known as the Civil Rights Act of 1968, it became law on April 11, seven days after Martin Luther King died.

As the 1960s came to a close, African Americans still struggled. Old laws had been changed and new laws passed, yet many blacks could see little improvement

One day before his assassination, Martin Luther King Jr. stands with Jesse Jackson (second from left) and other civil rights leaders on the balcony of a Memphis motel.

in their own lives. Unemployment was still almost twice as high in the black community as it was among whites. The gap between black and white incomes was narrowing, but the difference remained significant. But there was hope on the horizon.

By now African Americans were not looking so much to civil rights legislation or to militant groups to bring about change. Martin Luther King Jr. was gone, but a new generation of black leaders was emerging on the political scene. These leaders would guide the African-American community into the future.

A memorial service for King

Voter registration in New York City, early 1990s

8
NEW STRUGGLES

By the early 1970s, more and more black Americans came to believe that equal rights could best be achieved by working within the established political system. Even the Black Panthers, under their new leader Elaine Brown, began to pursue power through politics rather than through violent action.

All over the United States, African Americans became increasingly active in government and began to win significant political victories. In 1966 Edward Brooke of Massachusetts became the first black senator of the 20th century. One year later, President Johnson appointed Thurgood Marshall to the Supreme Court.

On the local level, Carl Stokes was elected mayor of Cleveland, Ohio, in 1967, and Richard Hatcher was elected mayor of Gary, Indiana. In 1973 three major American cities elected black mayors: Tom Bradley in Los Angeles; Maynard Jackson in Atlanta; and Coleman Young in Detroit.

The black politicians of the 1970s presented a new image. Gone were most of the militant leaders of the 1960s. In their places were skilled professionals—educators, attorneys, and businesspeople—who sought and won support from both black and white voters. This new breed of politicians came from the growing black middle class.

Racial discrimination still took many forms, though. Some of the most violent displays of prejudice came during court-ordered school busing programs. By busing white and black students to schools in different neighborhoods, educators tried to achieve racial balance in public schools. The response was particularly violent in Boston, Massachusetts, where white parents threw

Since the 1970s, college enrollment and graduation among African Americans have greatly increased.

stones and screamed racial slurs at black children arriving in white neighborhoods by bus.

Throughout the 20th century, African Americans had won many battles in the courts. But in June 1978, the U.S. Supreme Court handed down a controversial decision. The case of *Regents of the University of California v. Allan Bakke* involved a white man, Allan Bakke, who was rejected twice by the medical school at the University of California at Davis. The school's admissions policy included a quota system, which reserved 16 positions each year for minority applicants. Bakke charged that the school's policy discriminated against him on the basis of race. He claimed that he was rejected by the school in favor of less-qualified black candidates. The Court ruled in Bakke's favor and declared that the university's quota system was unacceptable.

By reserving places for minority students, the University of California was practicing a policy known as affirmative action. Affirmative action involves aggressive recruitment and training of minorities in schools and businesses. Despite the Bakke decision, affirmative action became an important tool in the 1970s that helped African Americans enter professions and institutions that might otherwise have been closed off to them.

During the 1970s, college enrollments among African Americans more than doubled. More scholars began to recognize and study the works of black writers, artists, educators, and historical figures. Black studies programs were established at many major universities. African Americans also entered professions such as engineering, medicine, and business in larger numbers. In August 1983, astronaut Guion S. Bluford became the first black person to travel in space.

Guion Bluford

Throughout the 1980s, African Americans were elected and appointed to powerful positions in local, state, and federal government. Harold Washington was elected mayor of Chicago in 1983. David Dinkins became mayor of New York in 1989. That same year, Colin Powell was named chairman of the Joint Chiefs of Staff. In this job, Powell was the principal military advisor to the president of the United States. Civil rights leader Jesse

Colin Powell

Jackson sought the Democratic presidential nomination in 1984 and 1988. Although he did not win the nomination, he was influential in shaping the Democratic platform during both elections.

Barriers and Building Blocks

The successes of the civil rights movement, black elected officials, and government action have been significant. But in the 1990s, the African-American community still faces disturbing issues. Nearly one-third of black

Jesse Jackson

Americans live below the poverty line, compared to about 11 percent of white Americans. The unemployment rate among blacks is twice that of whites. Those blacks who are employed earn only about 60 percent of what whites earn. The net worth of the average black household is one-tenth that of the average white household.

In the 1960s, presidential adviser Daniel Patrick Moynihan (later a New York senator) warned the nation that the black family was under extreme stress. Moynihan, who is white, was criticized heavily by black leaders at the time. But much of what he warned about has come to pass. Teenage pregnancy in the African-American community is at an all-time high. Often unmarried, many young black mothers drop out of school to raise their children. The number of single-parent households in the black community is also on the rise. The nuclear family and the extended family, the backbones of the black community with roots in African tradition, are under siege.

Nearly one-quarter of black men are in jail or in some way involved with the criminal justice system, such as on probation. This figure exceeds the number of black men in college. Many black teenagers belong to violent street gangs. For young black men aged 14 to 24, homicide is the number one cause of death.

Many members of the African-American community are disillusioned and angry. This anger is often expressed through rap music, a singing style that has become extremely popular with both black and white teenagers. Many people criticize "gangsta rap," claiming that rap lyrics degrade women and promote gun use and gang violence. Other people criticize white-owned record companies, which make millions of dollars producing and selling rap music. Supporters say that rappers do not promote violence, but are simply expressing the anger so prevalent in black society.

In April 1992, anger in the black community reached a breaking point. The year before, four white police officers had beaten Rodney King, a black man who led police on a high-speed car chase through a Los Angeles

The acquittal of four police officers in the Rodney King case set off a string of demonstrations in 1992.

Children in New York protest urban violence, early 1990s.

neighborhood. Although the beating was recorded on videotape, the officers were acquitted of criminal charges. With the announcement of the acquittal, minority citizens in South Central Los Angeles and other parts of the city attacked motorists, looted businesses, and burned buildings. The rioting lasted for several days.

While some politicians condemned the lawlessness, many others called the Los Angeles riots a rebellion against white oppression. In the wake of the riots, black and white leaders focused their attention on unemployment, police brutality, and other injustices suffered by African Americans. The search for solutions to these problems continues.

While blacks in the United States carry on their struggles, they are cheered by efforts to end apartheid—the policy of legal segregation and discrimination against blacks that has existed in South Africa since 1948. In April 1994, black South Africans voted in democratic elections for the first time. Nelson Mandela became the nation's first black president. Many prominent African Americans—actors Danny Glover and Angela Bassett, political leader Jesse Jackson, businessman Mackie McCloud, and others—lent a hand in South Africa as the new day dawned.

The Africans in America are about 30 years past their own apartheid—the legacy of legal segregation defeated by the civil rights movement. Blacks have won the right to use public facilities and have achieved political gains. But black people in the United States remain a long way from economic power. The black middle class is growing, but the ranks of the black poor are growing even faster. Poverty and despair are widespread in urban centers. In the years ahead, the challenge for African Americans will be to build economic strength and to fight poverty and unemployment.

Contributions to American Life

The Africans in America have made long-lasting contributions to American culture, often in the face of great adversity. These contributors are far too many to list in this book. The following section highlights only a few of the thousands of African Americans who have become leaders in their fields and professions.

A young Democrat at the party's 1992 convention

The American political scene is alive with black leadership, particularly in the Democratic Party. As

Illinois senator Carol Moseley-Braun

chairman of the Democratic National Committee, Ron Brown played a major role in the election of President Bill Clinton in 1992. Brown became secretary of commerce in the Clinton administration. Democrat Maxine Waters has become an influential member of Congress. She represents a large portion of South Central Los Angeles and is an aggressive proponent of African-American rights. Carol Moseley-Braun is the second African American elected to the U.S. Senate since Reconstruction and the first African-American woman. Elected from Illinois in 1992, Moseley-Braun has become an ardent advocate for the African-American community.

Traditionally dominated by whites, the business world is slowly opening its doors to African Americans. Reginald Lewis was one of the most successful African-American businesspeople in the United States before his death in 1993. He bought Beatrice Foods and created TLC Beatrice. This billion-dollar corporation is the largest black-owned company in the United States. Robert Johnson is the founder and president of Black Entertainment Television (BET). Listed on the New York Stock Exchange, BET is the only cable company owned by and providing programs for African Americans. It is very popular among African-American youngsters, who particularly like its music video programs. Fletcher Wiley, known as "Flash," is a Boston attorney and businessman. He is the first African American ever selected to head the Greater Boston Chamber of Commerce.

Joycelyn Elders

Other blacks have made their mark in science and medicine. Deborah Prothrow-Stith earned her medical degree at Harvard Medical School. She is now an assistant dean at the Harvard School of Public Health. Prothrow-Stith's book, *Deadly Consequences*, puts forth solutions to violence in American society. She has developed an antiviolence curriculum used by many school districts across the country. Joycelyn Elders became surgeon general of the United States in 1993, but lost her position after taking a controversial stand about sex education in 1994. She earned her medical degree at the University of Arkansas and served as director of the Arkansas Department of Health from 1987 to 1992. Mae Jemison holds the distinction of being the first African-American woman to travel in space. Before entering the space program, Jemison earned a medical degree from Cornell University and worked as a Peace Corps physician in West Africa. She served as an astronaut from 1987 to 1992.

African Americans have a long-standing presence in athletics and have achieved greatness in both team and individual sports. Barry Bonds is perhaps the best baseball player in the major leagues. He played for the Pittsburgh Pirates and then signed on with the San Francisco Giants in 1992. He has won three Most Valuable

Player awards. His father, Bobby Bonds, was a great ballplayer himself. The elder Bonds is now a first base coach for the Giants. Charles Barkley is an outstanding basketball player. After many years with the Philadelphia 76ers, Barkley signed on with the Phoenix Suns and led them to the NBA finals in 1993. He has been featured in many TV commercials, primarily for the Nike shoe company. Jackie Joyner-Kersee holds the world record in the heptathlon, a seven-event track-and-field contest. Born in East St. Louis, Illinois, Joyner-Kersee won gold medals at the Olympic Games in 1988 and 1992. In 1988 she formed the Jackie Joyner-

Charles Barkley

Kersee Foundation, dedicated to helping children in poor urban neighborhoods.

On the entertainment front, blacks are well represented in television, film, and music. Bill Cosby is a widely acclaimed comedian and actor. He began his career as a stand-up comic and in the late 1960s starred in *I Spy* on NBC TV. More recently, Cosby starred in *The Cosby Show,* one of the most popular and profitable television shows of all time, and *Cosby Mysteries* on NBC. Oprah Winfrey is a well-known talk-show host and actress. Born in Mississippi, she overcame childhood abuse and other obstacles to achieve great success in the world of entertainment. Winfrey hosts her own TV show, *Oprah,* and has appeared in movies. She lives in Chicago, where she runs a TV and film production company, Harpo. Actor Denzel Washington

Denzel Washington in the film Glory

Spike Lee

76

Oprah Winfrey

grew up in New Rochelle, New York. He now lives in Los Angeles. Washington's first film was the comedy *Carbon Copy*. He acted in the NBC TV drama *St. Elsewhere* for six years and has appeared in *Malcolm X, The Pelican Brief, Philadelphia*, and other films. Noted filmmaker Spike Lee has given us hit films such as *She's Gotta Have It, Do the Right Thing, School Daze, Mo' Better Blues, Malcolm X*, and *Crooklyn*. Lee attended Morehouse College in Atlanta. He lives in Brooklyn, New York.

The rap group Public Enemy first attracted attention in 1988, when their song "Rebel without a Pause" became an underground classic. The group's *It Takes a Nation of Millions* was one of the highest selling rap albums of the 1980s. Public Enemy presented a new sound and a new message to listeners—a message that taught about black history and black heroes. The group has influenced many types of musicians, ranging from other rap artists to rock bands. Public Enemy is revered today as one of the foremost pioneers of rap music.

Boyz II Men came onto the music scene with their widely acclaimed album *Cooley High Harmony* in 1991. The singing group instantly became a nationwide hit. Their success helped revive the popularity of the Motown record label, which originally produced some of the greatest black musicians of the 1960s. Boyz II Men has appeared on many television specials, including the *Soul Train* and Grammy award shows.

Boyz II Men

Whitney Houston

The daughter of famed soul singer Thelma Houston, Whitney Houston grew up in a musical household. She met singers such as Dionne Warwick and Aretha Franklin, who motivated her to pursue a career in the arts. Houston started her career as a model in the early 1980s. Her debut album *Whitney Houston* (1985) included such hits as "Saving All My Love For You" and "How Will I Know." She rocketed to stardom and is now one of the most highly paid entertainers in the world. In 1992 she had a starring role in the blockbuster movie *The Bodyguard*. Houston is married to R&B singer Bobby Brown, who started out in the singing group New Edition before embarking on his own solo career.

Many black writers have won high acclaim. Educated at Howard University and Cornell, Toni Morrison has won many awards including the Pulitzer Prize for fiction. She teaches at Princeton University and has written such novels as *Song of Solomon, Beloved,* and *Jazz.* Maya Angelou is an accomplished writer, actress, and activist. She teaches at Wake Forest University in North Carolina and is well-known for her autobiography *I Know Why the Caged Bird Sings* and other works. She recently captured the nation's attention when she wrote and read a poem in honor of the inauguration of President Bill Clinton in January 1993. Charles Johnson won the prestigious National Book Award for his novel *Middle Passage* in 1990. Johnson's gripping historical novel takes the reader from bawdy New Orleans onto a slave ship and high seas adventure.

Toni Morrison

Maya Angelou

Celebrating African-American Culture

The list of famous African Americans goes on and on, and new names are always being added. Perhaps more important than the famous black people in the United States, though, are the millions of ordinary African Americans who are working to improve their neighborhoods, schools, and communities. Much of this work involves celebrating African-American heritage and culture. Two holidays have special significance to black people.

Juneteenth is celebrated each year in mid-June. The holiday traces its beginnings to the Civil War and the Emancipation Proclamation. Although Abraham Lincoln issued the proclamation in 1863, Texas's black residents didn't get news of their freedom until two years later. On June 19, 1865, Union general Gordon Granger arrived in Galveston to subdue a Confederate force. When Granger told the former slaves of their freedom, they rejoiced in the streets. Juneteenth remembers this day of rejoicing. The holiday was celebrated in Texas for many years after the Civil War, but gradually faded out. In the 1970s, black Texans revived the holiday. Now it has spread throughout the nation and is celebrated with music, food, and parades.

African-style crafts and clothing are popular at stores and street fairs. More and more black Americans are celebrating their African roots.

A black-owned ice cream business, New York City

Another important African-American holiday is Kwanzaa, which begins on December 26 and lasts for seven days. Created in the 1960s in the United States, the holiday is based on a traditional African harvest festival. Each day of Kwanzaa is dedicated to one of seven principles: unity, self-determination, collective work and responsibility, cooperative economics, purpose, creativity, and faith. Throughout the holiday, family members join together to discuss the seven principles and to celebrate African-American culture. Kwanzaa ends with a feast, music, dancing, and commitments for the new year.

Juneteenth and Kwanzaa commemorate both the struggles of the Africans in America as well as their achievements and hopes for a bright future. The history of the Africans in America is filled with both suffering and triumph. The issues facing African Americans are complex; the obstacles are many. But the opportunities are great as well.

INDEX

ACKNOWLEDGMENTS photographs and illustrations used with permission of © Frances M. Roberts: pp. 2, 66, 67, 71, 72, 82, 83, 84; Laura Westlund: p. 6; Mexican Ministry of Tourism: p. 7; Kunsthistorisches Museum: p. 8; Independent Picture Service: pp. 9, 12, 15, 43, 47, 49 (top), 54 (bottom), 55 (top), 60; South African Information Service: p. 11; Library of Congress: pp. 16, 17, 27, 33 (top), 34, 36, 37; National Archives: pp. 18, 20, 22, 28, 38, 46, 48, 50, 52 (bottom), 58; Amistad Research Center, Tulane University, New Orleans, Louisiana: p. 19; Sophia Smith Collection, Smith College: pp. 23, 29 (J. N. Byron); Metropolitan Museum of Art, Gift of Charles Stewart Smith, 1884: p. 25; Chicago Historical Society: p. 26; Hargrett Rare Book and Manuscript Library, University of Georgia: p. 31; Georgia Department of Archives and History: p. 33 (bottom); Indiana Historical Society Library, C4238: p. 39; Virginia State Library and Archives: p. 40 (bottom); Moorland-Spingarn Research Center, Howard University: p. 40 (top); Schomburg Center for Research in Black Culture: pp. 41, 56, 64; Erik Overbey Collection, University of South Alabama Archives: p. 42; Office of the Congressman: p. 44; The Ring Book Shop, Madison Square Garden: p. 45; *TV Times:* p. 49 (bottom); NAACP: p. 52 (top); *Arkansas Democrat-Gazette:* p. 53; Birmingham Public Library Department of Archives and Manuscripts: p. 54 (top); UPI / Bettmann: pp. 55 (bottom), 57, 59, 63; Chicago Housing Authority: p. 61; *Washington Post* / D.C. Public Library: p. 65; NASA: p. 68; Department of the Army: p. 69 (top); National Rainbow Coalition: p. 69 (bottom); *Pioneer Press* / Richard Marshall: p. 70; Carol Moseley-Braun, United States Senator: p. 73; Abingdon Press: p. 74; SportsChrome East / West: p. 75; Hollywood Book and Poster: pp. 76 (both), 77, 79; Motown Records: p. 78; UCA Archives: p. 80 (bottom); © Maria Mulas: p. 80 (top); © Richard B. Levine: pp. 81, 88.

Front cover: © Richard B. Levine
Back cover: © Frances M. Roberts